the INTUITIVE TAROT WORKBOOK

the
INTUITIVE
TAROT
WORKBOOK

GUIDED EXERCISES TO
UNLOCK YOUR INTUITION
FOR EFFORTLESS READINGS

KATHLEEN MEDINA

CASTLE POINT BOOKS
NEW YORK

www.castlepointbooks.com

The Castle Point Books trademark is owned by Castle Point Publishing, LLC.
Castle Point books are published and distributed by St. Martin's Publishing Group.

ISBN 978-1-250-33976-8 (trade paperback)
ISBN 978-1-250-33977-5 (ebook)

Design by Melissa Gerber
Composition by Noora Cox
Edited by Jennifer Calvert
Images used under license by Shutterstock.com and Creative Market

Our books may be purchased in bulk for promotional, educational, or business use. Please contact your local bookseller or the Macmillan Corporate and Premium Sales Department at 1-800-221-7945, extension 5442, or by email at MacmillanSpecialMarkets@macmillan.com.

First Edition: 2024

10 9 8 7 6 5 4 3 2 1

Contents

Harness the True Power of Tarot

EVERYONE IS INTUITIVE—INCLUDING YOU! Intuition is a completely natural function of the human mind. We are all picking up intuitive information all the time, but most people don't realize it. That's because intuition isn't the flash of foreboding you see in movies. Instead, intuition is the soft, calm, guiding presence of higher awareness. It's a heightened, extrasensory perception that registers the subtle energies around you. And it's ready and waiting for you to put it to good use.

One of the best ways to both unlock your intuition *and* utilize it is by reading Tarot. Like intuition itself, this ancient divination tool works through symbolism. The rich imagery, archetypes, and structure of Tarot have been created to bring you into your intuitive mind. Using the cards, you can learn how to tap into that inner guidance system and strengthen it. Then, using that newly honed inner guidance system, you can go deeper into the wisdom of the cards to uncover answers to all of your most pressing questions.

With thoughtful information and exercises, *The Intuitive Tarot Workbook* helps you do both! Whether you've been reading Tarot for years or are new to the practice, you'll find everything you need to strengthen your connection to the cards for readings that are consistently clear, accurate, and insightful. All you need is an open mind.

YOU ARE INTUITIVE!

Worried you don't have what it takes? Think of a time when you had a gut feeling about something (positive or negative) that proved to be right. It happens more than you realize. For example, maybe you were introduced to someone by a friend and felt wary of them. There was no reason for it—your friend loved this person—but you just had a *feeling*. Later, it turned out that the person betrayed your friend. That was your intuition speaking to you.

Many of us have also experienced not listening to our gut and regretting it later. Maybe you felt like staying home instead of going to that social function only to end up with a flat tire. That might have been your intuition and not your introversion talking!

Reflecting upon these intuitive experiences can give you the push you need to start actively using your intuitive muscle. As you practice and it gets stronger, you will learn to trust it and even rely on it. Your intuition will never let you down; it is your closest friend and ally.

Your mind is another story. Your analytical brain is constantly processing data based on past experiences, trying to figure out whether or not you are safe. This logical, rational aspect of the mind certainly has its uses, but it's like a computer—binary. It's all 1s and 0s, black and white, past and future. It has nothing to do with what's happening *now*. Your intuition, on the other hand, sees into all of the gray areas and fully exists in the now. It is always present (in both senses of the word: in the moment *and* there with you). Tapping into it allows you to see the bigger picture.

RECOGNIZING YOUR INTUITION

We've all had those moments where our thoughts start racing, saying things like, "Oh my God. What should I do? Should I leave? Should I stay? I don't have a good feeling, but maybe I'm just being paranoid." That is **not** your intuition. That is your analytical mind reacting to a subtle intuitive sense that something is off—namely, freaking out about it.

You'll know when your rational mind has taken over not only by the rising anxiety levels but also because you're questioning the validity of what you are sensing. Intuition, on the other hand, is always neutral, never fearful or emotionally charged. Even when your intuition is sounding the alarm, it's doing so calmly, with a quiet certainty. The trick is learning how to listen to it. And that's exactly what we'll be focusing on.

THE PATH TO EFFORTLESS READINGS

Learning Tarot can feel overwhelming, but there's no need to memorize the meanings of its seventy-eight cards. The answers we seek are already within us; Tarot simply helps bring them into focus. *The Intuitive Tarot Workbook* uses Tarot to guide and hone your intuition through thoughtfully designed exercises. With a little practice—which is a big part of the fun—the process will become effortless. And by the end, your intuition will be guiding your readings.

First, we'll focus on intuitive practices. Once you understand how to open up the intuitive side of your mind, you'll discover a treasure trove of guidance that's always available to you. *And* you'll learn how to access it at will. Then we'll incorporate Tarot into the mix. Brief descriptions and insightful exercises make it simple to learn each card and, more importantly, what each card means for *you*. Before you know it, you'll be performing powerful readings with ease!

THE POWER OF WRITING

Step by step, this workbook will help you build your foundational knowledge of intuition and Tarot. But don't worry—It won't feel like homework. You will be interacting directly with the information in a way that feels organic and personal. And recording your perceptions, your senses, and your feelings will not only help you tap into your intuition but also give you some insight into the workings of your own complex, fascinating mind.

Writing is a powerful tool for accessing your intuition because it's a solitary, introspective process that allows you to focus internally. When you put your thoughts, ideas, and insights onto paper, you open up a channel of energy. And writing freehand—with good, old-fashioned pen and paper—activates the right hemisphere of the brain (the creative, intuitive side). That's exactly what you want. So let those thoughts and feelings flow freely onto the pages of this book and fuel your discovery.

Unlocking Your Intuition

WE PERCEIVE THE PHYSICAL WORLD THROUGH our five senses: sight, hearing, smell, taste, and touch. Our body receives signals through the corresponding sense organs that are then sent to our brain to process. But our sixth sense—our intuition—works a little differently. It picks up on energy that is finer than the physical senses can process. And although it's connected to the physical senses, it isn't routed through the analytical mind. Instead, it is pure and unfiltered.

Later in the book we'll practice quieting the mind and connecting to that energy directly. But for now, let's focus on getting to know the three main ways we sense it: through clairvoyance, clairaudience, and clairsentience. (These are French words that mean *clear seeing*, *clear hearing*, and *clear feeling*.)

Clairvoyance is the subtle sense of vision. It allows you to see energy, such as auras or the energy field around an object, as well as visions in the mind's eye. In certain cases, it also allows you to see ghosts or apparitions.

Clairaudience is the subtle sense of hearing. It allows you to hear guidance inside your mind. (This is different from your normal internal monologue.) You might also hear specific songs, lyrics, or symbolic sounds, such as bells ringing when you are wondering if an idea is right for you.

Clairsentience is the subtle sense of feeling or sensation. This is what most people think of as the "gut feeling." You have a tangible reaction in your body when you're considering a situation in your life, such as a warm feeling in your heart or a tight sensation in your lower back.

We all experience these subtle senses, but we may not recognize them. The following exercises will strengthen your awareness of them so that you can deepen your connection with your intuition and enhance your readings. These are simple practices, but they're not always that easy. Your mind is going to want to step in and edit, analyze, and process what you sense. Intuitive impressions come and go quickly, so trust the first thing that comes to you and write it down. In other words, don't let your mind get a hold of it! This is the start of separating the intuition from the analytical brain.

Calibrating the Subtle Senses

Over the next few pages, you'll begin to tap into your subtle senses with some freewriting. Try to let your senses take the lead rather than your thoughts. Practice these five exercises every day for the next week and you will be astonished how effortless it becomes. You'll also find that you look forward to learning what your inner guidance system has to say.

SEEING

Take a deep breath. Keep your eyes soft and unfocused as you scan your environment. What images stand out to you? Then close your eyes and look inwardly toward the area at the center of your forehead. What flashes there? Pictures? Symbols? Colors? Write down everything you see.

DAY 1

....

....

....

....

....

....

....

....

....

....

DAY 2

....

....

....

....

....

....

....

....

....

....

DAY 3

....
....
....
....
....
....
....
....
....
....

DAY 4

....
....
....
....
....
....
....
....
....
....

DAY 5

....
....
....
....
....
....
....
....
....
....
....
....

DAY 6

....
....
....
....
....
....
....
....
....
....
....
....

DAY 7

....
....
....
....
....

....
....
....
....
....

HEARING

Take another deep breath. Write down anything you hear. Is there a noise in your environment that jumps out at you? Bring your attention to the area between your ears. Is there a sound, word, or song you hear internally?

DAY 1

....

....

....

....

....

....

....

....

....

....

DAY 2

....

....

....

....

....

....

....

....

....

....

DAY 3

....

....

....

....

....

....

....

....

....

....

DAY 4

....

....

....

....

....

....

....

....

....

....

DAY 5

....
....
....
....
....
....
....
....
....

DAY 6

....
....
....
....
....
....
....
....
....

DAY 7

....
....
....
....
....
....
....
....
....

HAVE FUN WITH IT

Remember that there's no right or wrong answer here. This isn't a pop quiz; these are exercises. This is a chance to tune into yourself and practice using your natural gifts. So relax and have fun as your heightened awareness reveals an incredible world of energy all around you.

FEELING

Take a deep breath. Now write down everything you are feeling inside your body. These may be emotions, physical sensations, or simply thoughts. Don't think—just write.

DAY 1

....
....
....
....
....
....
....
....
....
....

DAY 2

....
....
....
....
....
....
....
....
....
....

DAY 3

....
....
....
....
....
....
....
....
....
....

DAY 4

....
....
....
....
....
....
....
....
....
....

DAY 5

....
....
....
....
....
....
....
....
....
....

DAY 6

....
....
....
....
....
....
....
....
....
....

DAY 7

....
....
....
....
....

....
....
....
....
....

**Time for a five-minute break!
Maybe get a cup of tea
or stand up and stretch.**

INTERPRETING

When you are ready to begin again, take a deep breath. Now look over what you wrote without thinking too hard. Do any impressions jump out at you? Certain perceptions will feel stronger than others. Do you notice any repeating themes?

DAY 1

....
....
....
....
....
....
....
....
....
....

DAY 2

....
....
....
....
....
....
....
....
....
....

DAY 3

....
....
....
....
....
....
....
....
....
....

DAY 4

....
....
....
....
....
....
....
....
....
....

DAY 5

....
....
....
....
....
....
....
....
....

DAY 6

....
....
....
....
....
....
....
....
....

DAY 7

....
....
....
....
....
....
....
....
....

"Get out of your head and into your heart. Think less, feel more."

—OSHO

SYNTHESIS

Which subtle sense felt easier? Vision? Hearing? Sensing? Which felt harder or not as natural?

DAY 1

....
....
....
....
....
....
....
....
....
....

DAY 2

....
....
....
....
....
....
....
....
....
....

DAY 3

....
....
....
....
....
....
....
....
....
....

DAY 4

....
....
....
....
....
....
....
....
....
....

DAY 5

....
....
....
....
....
....
....
....
....
....

DAY 6

....
....
....
....
....
....
....
....
....
....

DAY 7

....
....
....
....
....

....
....
....
....
....

At the end of the week, look over your answers and just notice if any patterns emerge. If any of the senses feel harder to access than the others, don't worry. This is showing you which sense is more natural and which takes more practice.

Getting to Know Tarot

TAROT ISN'T SOME MYSTERIOUS AND BEWILDERING craft. It is a book of symbolism. The iconography is designed to evoke your natural intuition. The right hemisphere of the brain governs intuition, creativity, and spatial intelligence. It works in symbols, color, design, and art. Tarot is simply speaking its language, bringing you into a conversation with your intuitive side.

Though Tarot has a somewhat dark, occult reputation, it doesn't hold any mystical powers of its own. The idea that it does came from the medieval Roman Catholic Church, which denounced Tarot, astrology, and similar nonreligious practices. So the cards remained underground until the 1500s, when they resurfaced in France and Italy as playing cards.

As a result, traditional Tarot decks are full of iconography from medieval Europe. You see towers, knights, emperors and empresses, characters dressed in attire from the Middle Ages, cobblestone villages, and flowering arbors. These images represent life at that time, but the cards also draw from ancient mystical and alchemical symbols that transcend the outer world and touch something much deeper.

There are many wonderful modern Tarot decks whose authors have drawn from the traditional but created their own interpretations and artistic renderings. Whichever deck you are attracted to or resonate with is the right deck for you! Later in the book, we will focus on the individual cards' meanings as we explore the major arcana and minor arcana, allowing you room to work with your deck. But we'll start by creating an intuitive foundation with Tarot's structure and symbolism.

In performing the following exercises, you will utilize both the logical left brain and the perceptive right brain. You'll build cognitive associations with the cards while also strengthening your intuition. Each time you work with your cards, start by closing your eyes, taking a few deep breaths, tapping into your intuitive senses, and setting an intention to grow in your practice.

A SHARED EXPERIENCE

The "collective unconscious" is a psychology term that describes the consciousness all humans share. It underpins the personal mind. All archetypes, symbols, and mythologies of Tarot come from this deeper level of awareness, which is why you'll find these aspects in cultures around the world throughout history.

Meeting the Majors

The twenty-two major arcana cards represent the larger archetypal themes in life. Twenty-two is a powerful number in numerology. It's referred to as the "master builder," which hints at the majors being the basic structural elements that illuminate the soul's evolutionary path as we walk this earth. They start with The Fool, which signifies a jumping-off point, and end with The World, which indicates a culmination of the journey. All the cards in between are the stepping stones along that path.

Of course, our lives don't just follow this nice, neat, sequential order. Different influences pop up at different times. The following exercises will help you grasp the overall journey of the major arcana cards. The visual impressions of witnessing the full circle create an imprint in your mind that you'll be able to draw upon later. And by creating intuitive associations with individual card's themes, you'll be able to perceive and interpret each card's role in future readings.

THE CIRCLE OF THE MAJOR ARCANA

It's time to grab your Tarot deck! Turn the cards face up and separate out the twenty-two major arcana cards. Next, lay them out in a big circle in numeric order, starting with The Fool and ending with The World (which will end up next to The Fool). This will give you a visual template of the overall structure, putting things into order in your mind's eye.

SEE THE BIGGER PICTURE

For the following exercises, avoid focusing on the individual cards. Instead, look at the whole circle, taking a wide-angle view of the story it tells.

What thoughts and impressions come to you when you look at the cards this way? Let them flow freely, without analyzing them.

....

....

....

....

....

....

....

What does seeing the beginning (The Fool) and the end (The World) of the deck next to each other evoke?

....

....

....

....

....

....

"The true Tarot is symbolism; it speaks no other language and offers no other signs."
—ARTHUR EDWARD WAITE

Write down three cards that create a feeling of unease for you.

1: ....

2: ....

3: ....

What makes you uncomfortable about each of the three cards you chose? (For example, is it the main iconography, the colors, the title?)

CARD 1	CARD 2	CARD 3
....	....	....
....	....	....
....	....	....
....	....	....

Now write down three cards that feel uplifting.

1: ....

2: ....

3: ....

What about each of these cards inspires you? Again, you're simply looking at the cards, not worrying about their meaning.

CARD 1	CARD 2	CARD 3
....	....	....
....	....	....
....	....	....
....	....	....
....	....	....
....	....	....
....	....	....
....	....	....

PICKING YOUR THEME

Look again at the circle of the major arcana. If you had to pick only one card to represent the overarching theme in your life, which would it be? If you are new to Tarot, simply go with your gut. Notice which cards you feel strongly attracted to or repelled by.

Which card jumps out at you?

....

What pulls you to this card?

....

....

Take the card out of the circle and study it. If this card could speak to you, what would it say? Take some time to delve into this. Don't think or analyze—just allow for stream-of-consciousness writing.

....

....

....

....

....

....

WHEN THE CARD CHOOSES YOU

For those who have been working with Tarot awhile, the card that represents your theme could be the one that seems to follow you around—an archetype that occurs regularly in your life or comes up often in the readings you do for yourself.

Meeting the Minors

The minor arcana cards of Tarot represent specific situations, thoughts, feelings, and people. These fifty-six cards are divided into four suits of fourteen cards each. Each suit represents an element and a particular area of day-to-day life. Pentacles (earth) are material reality, money, and physicality. Swords (air) represent the mind—thoughts and beliefs. Wands (fire) deal with energy, action, and movement. Cups (water) are the emotional realm, feelings, and relationships.

There are ten numbered cards in each suit, followed by four court cards: page, knight, queen, and king. The aces (one) are the seed cards of each suit; they are the pure energy of the element, which builds in complexity until card number ten. The court cards represent individual people or personality characteristics. The page signifies a young person or someone with youthful energy. The knight represents a young adult or someone with a lot of energy and focus. The queen can signify a woman or the feminine qualities of the particular suit. The king can represent a man or the mature masculine aspects of a suit.

In many ways, Tarot is about pattern recognition. When you understand the basic structure of the minor arcana, it becomes much easier to intuitively relate to each card. That's what we'll be working on in the following exercises. (This will also help offset the daunting task of trying to learn fifty-six separate cards.)

THE FOUR COLUMNS

You're going to need some space for this exercise. Turn your Tarot deck face up and separate out the fifty-six minor arcana cards. Organize them into four piles by suit. Now create four columns—one for each suit—in numeric order, with the ace at the bottom and ten at the top. Then add the court cards to the top of each column: page, knight, queen, then king. Really spread out the cards so you can see each of them.

Step back and take a big-picture view of the cards. Do you see patterns in the symbolism? (For example, notice how all the aces convey the core nature of the element their suit represents.)

....

....

....

....

....

....

Spend some time just taking in the four columns. Then write down any impressions you get, allowing them to flow through you stream-of-consciousness style. Write down whatever comes to you.

....

....

....

....

....

....

"Whatever the cards show you, always trust the words that well inside you."

—GWENDOLYN WOMACK

THE SUITS

Next, let's focus on one column at a time. Let yourself be immersed in each suit and write any thoughts that come to you about it. How does the iconography of each suit speak to you? What does its element evoke? Just write freely.

CUPS

....

....

....

....

....

....

....

SWORDS

....

....

....

....

....

....

PENTACLES

....
....
....
....
....
....

WANDS

....
....
....
....
....
....

A GAME OF CARDS

Playing cards evolved from the minor arcana of Tarot. Cups became hearts, wands became clubs, swords became spades, and pentacles became diamonds. From the court cards, pages and knights merged into the jacks of each suit.

Now let's focus on the court cards. This exercise is about identifying the court card that you feel describes you. You'll do this by matching not only your age and general nature (as described on page 28) but also your astrological sun sign with a card. This will deepen your sense of intuition about the individual characteristics of the court cards and help you glean their meanings in future readings.

Your sun sign is based on your birth date—it's your answer when someone asks, "What is your sign?" Each sign is associated with an element, just like the suits in Tarot. Aries, Leo, and Sagittarius are fire signs, which correspond to wands. Taurus, Virgo, and Capricorn are earth signs—pentacles in Tarot. Gemini, Libra, and Aquarius are air signs, or swords. And Cancer, Scorpio, and Pisces are the water signs, which correspond to cups.

> ## "To make the Tarot speak is our objective, but the arcana only speak to those who have learned to understand them."
>
> —OSWALD WIRTH

MY SUN SIGN:

....

Lay out the four court cards of the suit associated with your element. What patterns do you notice in their imagery?

....

....

....

....

....

....

MY SUIT:

....

The suits give you information about your predominant way of operating in the world. Do you lead with your intuition and feeling sense (cups)? Are you someone who approaches life through your mental faculties (swords)? Are you more action oriented (wands)? Or more comfortable dealing with material reality (pentacles)?

....

....

....

....

....

....

....

MY AGE:

....

If you are a young person or still considered a dependent, you are a page. If you are independent and focused on finding your path in the world, you are a knight. If you are an adult with a bit of wisdom and experience, you are a queen or king. How do you identify with your place in the court?

....

....

....

....

....

....

....

....

....

GENDER IN THE CARDS

Pages and knights are gender-neutral representations, but queens and kings are not. Queens are associated with women and archetypal feminine characteristics, and kings are associated with men and male characteristics. This can help you associate specific people with these cards in a reading based on an individual's gender identity.

MY COURT CARD:

....

Study your card. Write down the characteristics that jump out at you.

....

....

....

Do you personally relate to some of the symbols? If so, how?

....

....

....

How do you connect with the element of your court card?

....

....

....

What aspects of this element do you see in your basic nature?

....

....

....

**Working through this exercise with yourself in mind
can help you understand and identify anyone's court-card
characteristics. So have some fun relating to the court cards!**

Repeat the exercise, this time thinking about people you know well. This will help you later when these cards come up in a reading.

Who are you reading?

....

Consider their sun sign, suit, and age. Which card best represents them?

....

....

....

Study the card. Write down the characteristics that jump out at you.

....

....

....

....

....

....

Do any of the symbols feel like them? If so, how?

....

....

....

....

....

What aspects of their element do you see in their basic nature?

....

....

....

....

....

TAROT BY THE NUMBERS

Wondering about the numbers on the cards? Numerology, which is the esoteric science of numbers, also factors into Tarot in both the minor and major arcana. Each number carries particular properties, but how they apply to a reading depends on the context of the cards within the reading. Here are a few possible interpretations:

0: The Divine, freedom, and potential

1: Beginnings, independence, and leadership

2: Harmony, relationships, and indecision

3: Beauty, optimism, and drama

4: Practicality, material goods, and caution

5: Communication, travel, and change

6: Family, responsibility, and loyalty

7: Introspection, solitude, and studiousness

8: Ambition, success, and courage

9: Culmination, idealism, and wisdom

10: Beginnings, transition, and renewal

Understanding the Major Arcana

THE MAJOR ARCANA OF TAROT REPRESENT THE BIG themes in life. They follow the hero's journey from the beginning (The Fool) to the end (The World). When a major arcana card shows up in a reading, it indicates the theme you are working with at that time. Keep this in mind as you begin to dive into understanding each card. Its guidance is not just situational; it is thematic. Major arcana cards are also stronger, in a sense, than minor arcana cards, and their influence will cover a longer span of time (usually six months).

Different decks represent these overarching themes in different ways, depending on the author's perspective. However, their basic underlying messages are the same for all decks. In the following exercises, you will work on intuiting what these themes mean for you. This helps you establish a personal relationship with each card that will give you a foundation to work from when you see it in a reading. Coupled with your knowledge of the card's basic meaning, your intuitive associations will create richer readings.

0 · THE FOOL

This card represents powerful new beginnings and being divinely guided. It tells you: "Don't think, just jump!"

Study The Fool card. What symbolism jumps out at you? Does the imagery support this as being a positive thing? Something you can trust?

....

....

....

....

What does the idea of doing something "foolish" evoke in you?

....

....

....

....

Think of a time when you felt really inspired to start something new. It may not have made logical sense, but your heart and your intuition were telling you to go for it. This could have been deciding to begin a new career, take a big trip, or make a major lifestyle change. What did this feel like? How were you able to overcome self-doubt and take action?

....

....

....

....

....

....

....

....

I · THE MAGICIAN

The Magician signifies divine inspiration, powerful modes of communication, and bringing ideas into manifestation.

Study The Magician card. How do the symbols speak to you?

....
....
....
....

What does it mean to you to turn thought into action?

....
....
....
....

Do you have an idea that you would like to bring to life? Is there something you've been wanting to communicate to someone? Do you have a story to tell, or a work of art you want to create? Is there some project that you dream about one day actualizing? Write about it, allowing space for divine inspiration.

....
....
....
....
....
....

"As above, so it is below."

—HERMES TRISMEGISTUS, *THE EMERALD TABLET*

II · THE HIGH PRIESTESS

This card evokes intuition, a strong inner voice, independence, and emotional equipoise. You have access to your internal guidance system—use it. This inner temple is not of this world.

Study The High Priestess card. In what way is the imagery evocative of the power of the feminine?

....

....

....

....

There is a mysteriousness to this card. What symbols indicate this?

....

....

....

....

True inner guidance exists independently of outside influences. Recall a time when you had a strong intuitive knowing about a situation. What did that feel like? How did you listen to this inner guidance?

....

....

....

....

....

Next time you feel it, will you be willing to sit with this sense of inner knowledge? Visualize yourself doing so.

III · THE EMPRESS

This card indicates that this is a fruitful time for you. Abundance, fecundity, creativity, and beauty are present in your life. This is a time to acknowledge what is manifesting around you.

Study The Empress card. How do the colors speak to you? Do you sense the richness in the imagery?

....

....

....

....

Does she inspire a feeling of abundance in you? How is that showing up in your life right now?

....

....

....

Follow your desire to bring something wonderful into your life. Write about ways you can honor this desire. For example, are you taking time to enjoy what you have created or are in the process of creating? Can you make your surroundings more beautiful? How?

....

....

....

....

....

LISTEN TO THE EMPRESS

When you see this card, spend some time in nature. You could tend to your own garden or go to a botanical garden. Just immerse yourself in natural beauty.

IV · THE EMPEROR

Seeing The Emperor in a reading indicates that it is time for action. This card signifies taking charge, asserting authority, initiating projects, and working on goals that matter to you.

Study The Emperor card. Is the imagery more masculine than the Empress card? In what ways? Can you sense the energy of power in this card?

....

....

....

In what ways do you feel strong? Do you feel comfortable taking charge in situations that call for it?

....

....

....

....

This card is a message to move forward on something you want to build. What might that be for you? In your career? In a relationship? A literal structure?

....

....

....

....

Take a moment and imagine yourself as the Emperor, seated on your throne. Take a deep breath, then visualize yourself taking action and confidently accomplishing your goal.

The traditional meaning of this card is religious in nature; it indicates ceremonies, weddings, and rites of passage. The Hierophant is about bringing the spiritual into the physical.

Study The Hierophant card. Is there a spiritual teacher or teachings that come to mind? This could be through your faith, or it could be secular. How do you feel the presence of this in the imagery?

....

....

....

....

....

....

....

In what ways can you broaden your spiritual horizons? What does bringing more consciousness into your present life look like for you? Is there a person with whom you wish to study? Are you thinking of going to Bible study or of starting a yoga or meditation practice? Are you looking forward to a ceremony, either for yourself or another? Write about what calls to you.

....

....

....

....

....

....

....

....

....

....

VI · THE LOVERS

This card indicates that it's time for passion! This might mean deepening an existing relationship or, if single, awaiting the arrival of a new love relationship.

Study The Lovers card. What sensations come to you? Excitement? Fear? Hope? Longing?

....

....

....

....

What does intimacy mean to you? In what ways can you bring more honesty and intimacy into your life?

....

....

....

....

How can you think less and feel more?

....

....

....

....

....

Is there someone you've met recently to whom you're attracted? How does that feel in your body?

....

....

....

....

....

VII • THE CHARIOT

The Chariot signifies that you are in a time of preparation, getting ready for a new journey. This is a meditative, introspective process. Take stock and get organized.

Study The Chariot card. Take some time to sense and write about what it symbolizes for you.

....

....

....

What about this card evokes calm introspection?

....

....

....

What new journey—literal or metaphorical—have you been contemplating? In this instance, what does "preparation" mean for you?

....

....

....

Do you feel impatient? If so, how can you focus on what needs to be done now? Do you have any unfinished business or loose ends that you can tie up? Take a few moments to write this down.

....

....

....

Consider whether you feel better or calmer having a plan in place.

VIII · STRENGTH

This card indicates tapping into your power. It's time to tune into your own strength. Welcome and embrace your inner lion—take deep breaths into your belly and roar!

Study the Strength card. Notice the colors and symbolism. Let the card's energy awaken your fire. What does it inspire in you?

....

....

....

....

What does "strength" mean to you? Write down five specific characteristics you have that embody this.

....

....

....

....

Meditate on how you can employ these qualities in your life or even in a specific current situation. It could be as simple as exchanging negative beliefs for positive affirmations. (For example, try saying "I am unstoppable" to yourself until you believe it!)

IX · THE HERMIT

The Hermit symbolizes the spiritual seeker. This is a time to follow the path less traveled and let your inner light guide you. You don't need to explain yourself or be understood by others.

Study The Hermit card. What does the imagery invoke in you? Does the idea of following your own path scare you or comfort you?

....
....
....
....
....

At this time in your life, are you contemplating walking in a direction that is different from the people around you? How does this make you feel? Are you afraid of being alone?

....
....
....
....

Write the word "autonomy." Then journal about any feelings this word evokes.

....
....
....
....

How would you act if you trusted yourself to follow your own path?

....
....
....
....
....

X · THE WHEEL OF FORTUNE

The Wheel of Fortune signifies good luck and right timing. External changes for the better are on the horizon. This is a period of increased opportunity and expansion.

Study The Wheel of Fortune card. How do the symbols convey positive change? Can you sense the theme of increased activity and movement?

....

....

....

....

Do you believe in luck? Why or why not?

....

....

....

....

Are you hoping for more opportunity in a certain area of your life? What would this look like? An expansion in your business? Buying or selling a house? Moving to another location? Would you like greater possibilities in your personal life, such as meeting new people or taking a current relationship to another level? Write about the changes you'd like to see.

....

....

....

....

....

....

....

....

XI · JUSTICE

This card represents balance, thoughtfulness, and discernment. It is a time to weigh options and consider what is best. Detachment and solemnity—not emotional reactions—will help you now.

Study the Justice card. How do the images and colors convey equilibrium? Do you sense the energy of calmness, balance, and non-reactivity?

....

....

....

....

If you have a decision you've been struggling with, start a list of pros and cons here.

....

....

....

Consider the situation, or even your life overall, and check in with yourself. Is it possible you need to adjust something to achieve more equanimity? What would bring you balance?

....

....

....

....

REPEATING DIGITS

Double-digit numbers are called Master Numbers in numerology because they are powerful in amplifying a theme. In the case of the Justice card, the number eleven gives the card's message of harmony a boost. Use the clarity it offers to your advantage.

XII · THE HANGED MAN

This card is your sign to let go. Surrender your situation to the wisdom of a higher power (in whatever way that has meaning for you).

Study The Hanged Man card. As you look at its powerful symbolism, what feelings arise?

....

....

....

....

What does the concept of "surrendering" mean to you?

....

....

....

....

This card indicates that it's time to release fixed agendas, to allow the Universe to step in and move you in the right direction. Are you hanging on to something for dear life? If so, why?

....

....

....

....

Can you let go of your desire for a certain outcome and make room for something better? Write five sentences that begin with "I now release . . ." Then take a breath and feel the relief that comes with letting go.

....

....

....

....

XIII · DEATH

This card in **not** a signifier of physical death! It represents profound transformation—the end of some situation in your life that will foster a new beginning.

When most people see this card, it makes them uncomfortable. How does the iconography of this card speak to you?

....

....

....

....

Does the idea of death scare you? What feelings does it evoke?

....

....

....

Death is a natural process, releasing old forms to create new ones. In what area of your life do you sense an ending is at hand? Write down what this change would mean. If this longtime situation comes to a close, what else could be possible?

....

....

....

....

"The secret of life is to 'die before you die'–and find that there is no death."

—ECKHART TOLLE

XIV · TEMPERANCE

The Temperance card indicates integration, internal wholeness, and well-being. It can also imply the union of the masculine and feminine aspects of your personality. You are entering a time of deeper psychological awareness.

Study the Temperance card. What are the illustrations conveying to you? How do they represent the union of opposites?

....

....

....

....

When you draw this card, it signifies a time to look within for wholeness and answers. Write down five aspects of your personality that you consider negative.

....

....

....

....

Now write down five aspects of your personality that you feel are positive.

....

....

....

....

How do these traits relate to each other? Can you recognize how accepting all aspects of yourself will lead to greater well-being?

....

....

....

....

XV • THE DEVIL

This card is one of the most misunderstood in Tarot. The Devil does not symbolize an outside force of evil that you are powerless to fight—unless you think you are! Something or someone is testing you.

Study The Devil card. What fears does it evoke in you? Are you feeling powerless in some area of your life?

....

....

....

This card can indicate that it's time to step back and become aware how social conditioning is imprisoning you. How do your belief systems either empower you or keep you from believing in yourself?

....

....

....

How can you take charge of your mind?

....

....

....

If you're struggling with something, write down some steps you can take to free yourself.

....

....

....

**You are stronger than your fears!
Meditate on the mantra "I am not afraid."**

XVI · THE TOWER

The Tower signifies the breakdown of an outmoded structure. But this is a healing crisis—essentially, burning down the house to replace it with a stronger structure. Clearing one situation allows for a much healthier one to take its place.

Study The Tower card. Tap into what this symbolism means for you. What structures are represented for you? What is happening as you envision these structures collapsing?

....

....

....

....

....

....

Take a deep breath and look directly at what situation in your life needs to change. Is there an internal or external structure you have been wanting to walk away from? Is there something that you know you need to deal with but are scared to because you've been in it for so long? Maybe it's a toxic belief system, a relationship, or a job. Identify what is negatively impacting you and write about how much better life could be without it.

....

....

....

....

....

....

....

....

....

....

....

XVII · THE STAR

The Star is a card of inspiration, peace, and clarity. It offers a clear vision of future possibilities, an epiphany that can lead you forward.

Study The Star card. Mediate on its imagery. How do the symbols make you feel? Can you sense the energy of clarity and guidance in this card?

....

....

....

....

Have you recently had a bold new idea? Is something inspiring you? In what way does that idea indicate a new direction for you?

....

....

....

This is a time to be open to either a lightning bolt of insight or the gradual rising of a guiding star. Either way, it will light up the night sky of your mind. Close your eyes, take a deep breath, and ask for guidance. Now write down any symbols, visions, or feelings that arise.

....

....

....

....

ENLIGHTENING IMAGERY

Many decks portray The Star as a woman pouring water from two cups—a suit of the minor arcana tied to emotion. This symbolizes emotionally nourishing guidance.

XVIII · THE MOON

The Moon symbolizes the seductive power of the subconscious. This card cautions you not to get sucked into your old patterns. Steer clear of the past and break unhelpful habits.

Study The Moon card. It holds clues to the workings of the subconscious and indicates how to walk ahead toward the future instead of turning back toward the past. What do you sense from it?

....

....

....

....

This card serves as a warning that you are tempted to go back to some way of thinking or acting that doesn't serve you anymore. Take a moment to consider how you might be doing the same old thing and hoping for a different result. What does that mean for you right now?

....

....

....

....

Write down any old patterns you're still acting out. Are any of them no longer serving you? How?

....

....

....

....

....

Now write about what it would look and feel like to do something different. (And then follow that path!)

....

....

....

This card signifies that a new day and a new dawn are at hand. It's a bright indicator of happiness and fulfillment and an optimistic new perspective that you can trust.

Study The Sun card. Take in its imagery. How do the colors and symbols speak to you? Do they evoke a sense of well-being?

....

....

....

....

What does it feel like to contemplate a metaphorical sunny day?

....

....

....

Look around at your environment and write down what you are grateful for.

....

....

....

Meditate on the positive aspects all around you. Is there a situation that is making you happy and excited? If so, write about it. If not, write down what would make you happy.

....

....

....

Now rest in the certainty that some version of what you are hoping for is making its way into your life.

XX · JUDGMENT

The Judgment card is about objectivity, seeing things as they really are. It signifies an opportunity to understand your life or a situation from a higher perspective.

Study the Judgment card. Which symbols speak to you? Do you get a sense of freedom? How does looking at the imagery give you a higher perspective?

....

....

....

....

What does the idea of objectivity mean for you right now?

....

....

....

....

When this card comes up, it says that a level of detachment and good judgment are available to you. Try to step outside a situation you're struggling with, as if you were an observer. How does it change your perspective?

....

....

....

....

If a friend were in your situation, asking for your advice, what would you say to them? Write this down.

....

....

....

....

XXI • THE WORLD

The World signifies coming full circle—completion, favorable endings, and new beginnings. This card tells you you're at one with the Universe and enjoying a higher consciousness.

As you study the imagery in The World, what feelings does it invoke? Spend some time meditating on the symbols and their deeper meanings.

....

....

....

....

This card indicates that the events in your life are in harmony with the Universe. If you are not feeling that currently, write about what it would feel and look like for you.

....

....

....

....

Can you trust that things are coming together for you? Why or why not?

....

....

....

....

. . . .

**This card signifies that things are falling into place.
Take some time to visualize this and feel good about it!**

Understanding the Minor Arcana

MINOR ARCANA CARDS GIVE YOU INFORMATION

about specific situations and people. Each of the four suits (swords, cups, wands, and pentacles) are numbered one (ace) through ten, offering a variety of details that enhance your reading. And each court card (page, knight, queen, and king) offers insight into the personality traits of an individual. But understanding the element of each card you are working with is the key to understanding its message.

The exercises in this section study each suit from beginning (ace) to culmination (king). By the end, you will have the meaning of each element securely anchored in your consciousness. Using intuition to build personal associations with the elements and the cards will allow you to understand the nature of each card when you see it in a reading and ensure an accurate and illuminating interpretation.

ACE OF SWORDS · ACE OF CUPS · ACE OF WANDS · ACE OF PENTACLES

BUILD ON YOUR WORK

Once you've finished these exercises, you can refer back to them during readings. This will help strengthen the intuitive connection you're creating here.

ACE OF SWORDS

The Ace of Swords is the seed card of the air element, representing the power and potential inherent in this element. The Ace of Swords signifies an inspiration or a clear new idea.

What do you sense when you look at this card?

....

....

....

What does clarity mean to you?

....

....

....

How does it feel when you have a bold new idea?

....

....

....

Consider an epiphany you've had. What qualities did this have for you?

....

....

....

....

THE SUIT OF SWORDS

Swords symbolize the air element, which is associated with the realm of thought, ideas, and beliefs.

The Two of Swords is about indecision and being caught between two seemingly opposing ideas.

What do you sense when you look at this card?

....

....

....

What decision do you find yourself struggling with currently? Write out the two opposing thoughts or beliefs you're struggling with.

....

....

....

....

....

Imagine you already know what to do. Write out, in detail, what that would look like.

....

....

....

....

....

....

....

....

How does that solution feel?

....

....

....

THREE OF SWORDS

The Three of Swords signals that your thoughts are actively going against your heart.

What do you sense when you look at this card?

....
....
....

Take a moment and put your right hand over your heart. Take three deep breaths. Ask your heart to speak to you. Write out what it says.

....
....
....
....
....

How might your thoughts be hurting you or holding you back presently? How are your thoughts opposing what your heart is telling you?

....
....
....
....
....
....

"Quiet the mind, and the soul will speak."

—MA JAYA SATI BHAGAVATI

FOUR OF SWORDS

The Four of Swords indicates postponement. Use it as an opportunity to center yourself.

What do you sense when you look at this card?

....

....

....

What situation in your life seems to be on hold?

....

....

....

....

....

This card tells you it is a good time to take a mental break, to allow yourself a time of postponement. What can you do to give your mind a break from worrying about moving things forward? (For example, you could meditate.)

....

....

....

....

....

....

Now write "Don't think, just relax" as many times as it takes to sink in.

....

....

....

....

....

FIVE OF SWORDS

The energy of the Five of Swords is about self-doubt and self-denigration. Mental agitation is wearing you down.

What do you sense when you look at this card?

....
....
....

Imagine your mind is like a glass of muddy water, and the more you think, the murkier it gets. Visualize yourself setting the glass down and allowing the sediment to settle. Then write about any self-doubt you have at this time.

....
....
....
....
....

Now write out how you can let things settle down.

....
....
....
....
....

Is there still as much doubt? Does your mind feel a bit calmer? What else has changed?

....
....
....
....
....

SIX OF SWORDS

The Six of Swords signifies a chance to gain some awareness about how societal beliefs have been steering the ship.

What do you sense when you look at this card?

....

....

....

Write down any expectations or beliefs that your family members or others close to you have about how you should behave.

....

....

....

....

....

Take a moment and imagine what it would be like if you let these go. Write about what that would look and feel like.

....

....

....

....

....

If you were to choose to follow your own beliefs, what would these be?

....

....

....

....

....

SEVEN OF SWORDS

The Seven of Swords indicates that someone is not being truthful. This could be you, lying to yourself or putting on a mask to hide your real thoughts.

What do you sense when you look at this card?

....

....

....

Are you being honest with yourself and others about what you really think? Write down any ways in which you are hiding your truth right now.

....

....

....

....

....

Is there someone in your life you think is not being honest? Write out why this may be the case.

....

....

....

....

"At the center of your being
you have the answer;
you know who you are and
you know what you want."

—LAO-TZU

EIGHT OF SWORDS

The Eight of Swords represents thinking there is something wrong you or being bound by feelings of guilt, shame, or unworthiness.

What do you sense when you look at this card?

....

....

....

Take a deep breath, then write a list of what you think you have done wrong or are doing wrong.

....

....

....

....

....

....

As you look over the list, give yourself grace. Then rewrite the list by beginning each entry with the words, "I now let go of . . ."

....

....

....

....

....

....

How do you feel? Can you sense a bit more spaciousness in your mind?

....

....

....

....

NINE OF SWORDS

The Nine of Swords is the "nightmare card." It signifies being chased by a terrifying monster lurking in the psyche: old core fears that produce anxiety.

What do you sense when you look at this card?

....

....

....

What are the core fears that keep you up at night? Take a moment to commit to looking directly at these fears, then write them out. Keep the pen moving until you can't find anything else that scares you. (Use a separate piece of paper if you need more space.)

....

....

....

....

Now spend some time thinking about how you can dispel those fears. With logic? With comfort? By sharing them with others? Write out your solutions.

....

....

....

....

A MINOR INCONVENIENCE

Keep in mind that these are minor cards, which means that any negative situations are temporary. The trick is to look for ways to move through them.

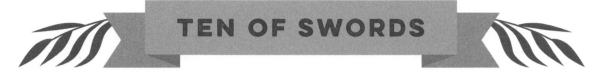
The Ten of Swords signifies the death of a way of thinking and letting go of an old perspective once and for all.

What do you sense when you look at this card?

....

....

....

In what ways are you "sick and tired of being sick and tired"? Write these down.

....

....

....

....

....

What situation in your life at this time might be triggering this?

....

....

....

....

....

....

Write "I'm officially done with this way of thinking" until you truly feel ready to let go and move on.

....

....

....

....

....

PAGE OF SWORDS

The Page of Swords signifies an agile but restless mind—thoughts bouncing around all over the place. It can also represent a person who is quick thinking and has a youthful mental energy—or seeing these characteristics within yourself.

What do you sense when you look at this card?

....

....

....

Take an honest look at yourself. Is your mind jumping around? Do you feel ungrounded? What makes you feel this way?

....

....

....

....

Take three deep breaths. Write down the thoughts going through your mind at this time.

....

....

....

....

Now that your thoughts are on paper, how does your mind feel?

....

....

....

....

....

ASTROLOGICAL ASSOCIATIONS

The suit of Swords is associated with the sun signs: Gemini, Libra, and Aquarius. If one of its court cards indicates a person in your life, they likely are one of these signs or exhibit its characteristics.

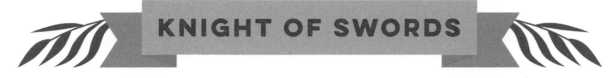

KNIGHT OF SWORDS

The Knight of Swords signifies thinking in a manner that is guarded, defensive, or aggressive. It can also represent a person with forceful or powerful focused mental energy—or seeing these characteristics within yourself.

What do you sense when you look at this card?

....

....

....

Write about an idea or belief that you strongly identify with now.

....

....

....

....

....

Does this belief cause you to be defensive or act out in a negative way? If so, why?

....

....

....

....

....

How can you be less reactive? Write out some ways you can do this. This could include slowing down, trusting that you'll get to where you need to go easily, and believing that the answers will come to you.

....

....

....

....

QUEEN OF SWORDS

The Queen of Swords indicates being emotionally detached—thinking instead of feeling. It can represent a woman who is aloof and analytical, sometimes even cold and unsympathetic, but also capable of astute awareness. It can also signify seeing these characteristics within yourself.

What do you sense when you look at this card?

....

....

....

This card can indicate inheriting a strong belief system from your mother. Write down any perspectives, ideas, or belief structure you inherited from your maternal line or a strong female role model.

....

....

....

....

....

How does this help or hinder you in your present life?

....

....

....

....

What would it look like to trust your own perspective in your current situation?

....

....

....

....

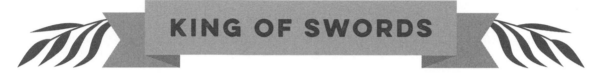

KING OF SWORDS

The King of Swords indicates great discernment and mental faculties but also control and authoritarianism. It can represent a potentially didactic and critical man with a strong intellect and disciplined approach to life—or seeing these characteristics within yourself.

What do you sense when you look at this card?

....

....

....

Take a moment to check in with yourself and see if your inner critic is present. What is it saying to you?

....

....

....

....

....

Is there a man in your life who is controlling? Do you feel threatened or intimidated by him?

....

....

....

....

....

....

How can you be your own authority figure?

....

....

....

....

ACE OF PENTACLES

The Ace of Pentacles is the seed element of earth. It represents a literal gift, a financial opportunity, or a new situation that is the beginning of positive growth.

What do you sense when you look at this card?

....

....

....

What new person, situation, or opportunity has shown up in your life recently?

....

....

....

....

What metaphorical seeds do you want to plant for the future?

....

....

....

Are you having trouble believing this new offer or opportunity is real? Or that it would be good for you? If so, write out why. Then give it a chance!

....

....

....

THE SUIT OF PENTACLES

Pentacles represent the earth element and all aspects of the material realm—money, physicality, and health.

The Two of Pentacles signifies a kind of limbo, but not in a bad sense. This is a time when things are in flux, so just stay present until your next move becomes clearer.

What do you sense when you look at this card?

....

....

....

Do you feel like you are stuck in some area of your life? Write it down.

....

....

....

....

Take a deep breath. How can you shift your perspective and trust more in divine timing? Can you find examples of it in your life?

....

....

....

....

....

**Keep it simple;
just do what is before you right now.**

THREE OF PENTACLES

The Three of Pentacles offers reassurance that you are making step-by-step progress. Slow and steady wins the race!

What do you sense when you look at this card?

....

....

....

What goal do you most want to achieve at this time?

....

....

....

....

....

Write down some small steps you can take every week toward reaching this goal.

....

....

....

....

....

. . . .

As you proceed, check off these steps and recognize your forward movement, no matter how small it seems.

FOUR OF PENTACLES

The Four of Pentacles indicates that you are contracting out of fear. But there is no need to batten down the hatches.

What do you sense when you look at this card?

....

....

....

In what ways might you be withholding? Are you being especially frugal? Not being open and honest in your relationships?

....

....

....

....

....

....

Recognize where fear is making you too cautious at this time. Write out your fears.

....

....

....

....

....

Take a breath, relax your shoulders. Now write down some ways you can be more generous with yourself or others.

....

....

....

....

The Five of Pentacles indicates survival-related fears or a situation in which you feel powerless. This might manifest in fears of poverty, scarcity, or being abandoned.

What do you sense when you look at this card?

....

....

....

Whatever this card triggers in you, honor it, then write it down.

....

....

....

....

....

Now take a step back, giving yourself space to allow for some insight. Every problem has a solution. How could you see this situation in a different light? Write down some ways to approach things from a new angle.

....

....

....

....

....

**Repeat the mantra,
"There is always a way forward."**

The Six of Pentacles represents security, staying in your comfort zone, and the temptation to compromise.

What do you sense when you look at this card?

....

....

....

Think about a situation you're currently dealing with in your life. Write down whatever comes to mind.

....

....

....

....

....

Now list the ways in which you are tempted to do what feels safer or more comfortable even when you know it is not what you really want.

....

....

....

....

....

Now, write out what you really want and consider how much better it feels!

....

....

....

....

....

SEVEN OF PENTACLES

The Seven of Pentacles signifies patience, allowing things time to gestate, and being positively expectant. There's no need to push.

What do you sense when you look at this card?

....

....

....

Is there something you want that you feel isn't happening fast enough?

....

....

....

....

....

Take a deep breath and write out some things you can do in the meantime to bring it about or give yourself a small piece of it now.

....

....

....

....

....

Ask yourself if you are generally a pessimist or an optimist. Can you see the benefit of optimism and of expecting good things to happen?

....

....

....

....

....

EIGHT OF PENTACLES

This card represents strong, steady growth. It points toward some material element that is healthy and secure and will produce results.

What do you sense when you look at this card?

....

....

Take a moment to observe what is happening in your life. Do you feel like all is evolving as it's meant to? How so?

....

....

....

Write about a situation that you have been nurturing over a period of time.

....

....

....

Now think back to when you started and write about all the progress you have made. How does this make you feel?

....

....

....

....

**Taking time to notice your gains helps alleviate
doubts that things will continue to fruition.**

NINE OF PENTACLES

The Nine of Pentacles signifies fruition. A situation has fully evolved, and you are ready to move to the next stage.

What do you sense when you look at this card?

....

....

....

What in your life do you feel really ready for? For example, maybe you've been studying a new technique in your work, and now it's time to implement it.

....

....

....

....

Write about what "fruition" means for you at this time.

....

....

....

....

How can you be more prepared for the next stage?

....

....

....

"When your intention is clear, so is the way."

—ALAN COHEN

TEN OF PENTACLES

The Ten of Pentacles is a great signifier of material gains, fulfillment, and success. It also indicates sharing the wealth with others.

What do you sense when you look at this card?

....

....

....

Take some time to acknowledge and celebrate where you are. What have you accomplished?

....

....

....

....

....

What do "abundance" and "fulfillment" mean for you presently?

....

....

....

....

....

In what ways are you inspired to share your abundance with others? By connecting with more people? By sharing your gifts, monetarily or in some other way? Or something else?

....

....

....

....

....

PAGE OF PENTACLES

The Page of Pentacles indicates a student and being in the stage of learning and growing in the outer world. It can represent a young person or a person who is learning a new skill, starting a new path, or being practical. It can also signify seeing these characteristics within yourself.

What do you sense when you look at this card?

....

....

....

Write down a few new things you are considering, such as learning a new skill, taking a class, or starting a new hobby.

....

....

....

If there is something you want to do but are reticent to begin, list your concerns.

....

....

....

....

....

ASTROLOGICAL ASSOCIATIONS

The suit of Pentacles is associated with the earth signs: Taurus, Virgo, and Capricorn. If one of its court cards indicates a person in your life, they likely are one of these signs or exhibit its characteristics.

Take a moment to close your eyes and imagine starting a new project. How does that feel in your body? (Hint: Don't listen to your mind!)

....

....

....

....

KNIGHT OF PENTACLES

All the knights of the minor arcana indicate action—in the case of the Knight of Pentacles, visible, steady, grounded progress. This card can represent a young adult, having the qualities of an apprentice or journeyman, or a person who moves toward the manifestation of their material goals. It can also signify seeing these characteristics within yourself.

What do you sense when you look at this card?

....
....
....

In what ways do you feel like you are making progress—or not making progress—toward a goal?

....
....
....
....
....

This card signifies a time of steady forward movement. What could you do to keep going?

....
....
....
....
....

What area of your life needs work? How can you engage more in this area? Write out what that would look like at this time.

....
....
....
....

QUEEN OF PENTACLES

The Queen of Pentacles is about beauty, luxury, and being in a more fruitful time in life. It can represent a woman with the earthy feminine qualities of fertility and sensuality. It can also signify seeing these characteristics within yourself.

What do you sense when you look at this card?

....

....

....

How can you spend more time on self-care? Could you get a massage? Buy a new outfit? Get creative!

....

....

....

....

....

Write about the beauty that currently exists around you. In what ways can you bring more of it to your environment?

....

....

....

....

Go somewhere lovely—a park, botanical gardens, out for a really good meal— and thoroughly enjoy yourself!

The King of Pentacles indicates good dealings with the material realm, creating financial security, and handling the practical aspects of life well. It can represent a man who is grounded, secure, and relaxed. It can also signify seeing these characteristics within yourself.

What do you sense when you look at this card?

....

....

....

This card signals that you can successfully take care of business. How are you doing that in your own life?

....

....

....

....

....

Think of a man in your life with these characteristics. How does he help you feel grounded?

....

....

....

....

How can you embody more balance and well-being in your material life?

....

....

....

....

....

....

THE ACE OF WANDS

The Ace of Wands is the seed card of this fiery suit. It signifies powerful new energy, enthusiasm, and the start of something that will propel you forward.

What do you sense when you look at this card?

....

....

....

What new energy is stirring within you right now?

....

....

....

....

THE SUIT OF WANDS

The Wands represent the fire element. Motivation, movement, and inspired action are all aspects of this suit.

What lights you up? What do you want more of in your life?

....

....

....

What action can you take to move forward on this desire?

....

....

. . . .

Close your eyes. Imagine a glowing flame in the center of your chest. See it getting bigger and bigger until it encompasses your whole body. Take a few moments to feel this energy.

TWO OF WANDS

The Two of Wands represents having options or seeing possibilities opening up that can further your growth. You are in a position to choose which direction you want to go.

What do you sense when you look at this card?

....

....

....

Take a few moments and look at what is going on in your life. How has a new option presented itself, either in the form of inspiration or in the physical world?

....

....

....

....

....

Write about the possibilities that you now see.

....

....

....

....

....

Trust that whatever option you choose will lead to the same destination. But, right now, which one feels better? Why?

....

....

....

....

....

THREE OF WANDS

The Three of Wands signifies a time of balance between various areas of life (e.g., personal, professional, and relationships). It offers a sense of ease, equipoise, and enjoyment.

What do you sense when you look at this card?

....

....

....

How does your life feel right now in terms of balance?

....

....

....

....

....

How do you maintain balance? Or, if you feel that your life could use more balance, write down some simple steps you believe would help you achieve this.

....

....

....

....

....

This card signals that it is a good time to scan your environment and observe what is transpiring in your world.

....

....

....

....

....

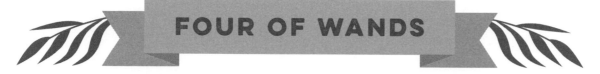

FOUR OF WANDS

This card indicates joyful interactions, positive participation with those close to you, and building solid relationships.

What do you sense when you look at this card?

....

....

....

Who are the people you are drawn to in your life now?

....

....

....

....

....

Write down three actions you can take to create better interactions and relationships with others.

....

....

....

....

**If you've recently spent a lot of time alone,
this card suggests that is changing.**

FIVE OF WANDS

The Five of Wands represents a time of strife or overwhelm when life feels chaotic. It tells you to slow down and take things easier.

What do you sense when you look at this card?

....

....

....

In what area of your life do you feel things are going a bit off the rails?

....

....

....

....

....

Take three deep breaths in through the nose and out through the mouth. Close your eyes and just sit for a few moments. Make a list of five things that you feel you need to take care of, in order of priority.

....

....

....

....

....

. . . .

 **Tackle this list one task at a time, taking care not to do more than is necessary.**

. . . .

SIX OF WANDS

The Six of Wands signifies victory, success in some area of life, and feeling more confident. Things are working out!

What do you sense when you look at this card?

....

....

....

Write about what "success" means to you right now.

....

....

....

....

Take a few moments to acknowledge what is going right in your life—or, at least, what's headed in the direction you'd like.

....

....

....

....

....

....

....

Repeat the mantra "I am successful in all my endeavors." Write it down if it makes it feel more real to you.

....

....

....

....

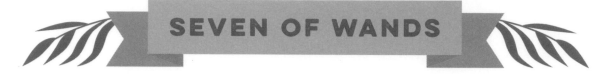

SEVEN OF WANDS

The Seven of Wands indicates that it's time to focus on yourself. Instead of taking care of others, prioritize your own needs.

What do you sense when you look at this card?

....

....

....

In what area of your life are you working too hard to meet the needs or demands of others?

....

....

....

....

How can you delegate more responsibilities to those around you?

....

....

....

Recognize that standing up for yourself benefits everyone. What can you do right now to empower yourself and, through you, others?

....

....

....

THE WISDOM OF THE AIRLINES

Remember, if the cabin of an airplane loses pressure,
you put your own oxygen mask on first. Only then
will you be able to assist those around you.

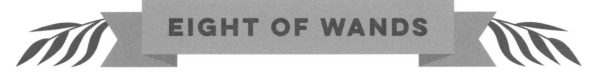

EIGHT OF WANDS

The Eight of Wands is the classic travel card. It signifies swiftness, effortless movement, and flowing action.

What do you sense when you look at this card?

....

....

....

Think about a trip you'd like to take. What do you hope to do and see?

....

....

....

....

....

What does taking action to move forward with your travel plans look like to you now? Write about how you can do this.

....

....

....

....

....

....

How does it feel to imagine yourself going on this journey?

....

....

....

....

....

NINE OF WANDS

The Nine of Wands indicates strength and great capabilities but also overworking and exhaustion.

What do you sense when you look at this card?

....

....

....

Take a moment to look at some area of your life where you may be overdoing it. Are you working too much? Putting too much effort into a relationship? What makes you feel like you have to do this?

....

....

....

....

....

What could you do to pull back a bit?

....

....

....

....

Write about what pulling back even just a little (say, 10 percent) would entail and how it would make you feel. Then turn it into a concrete action plan.

....

....

....

....

....

TEN OF WANDS

The Ten of Wands represents a kind of boiling point marked by anger, frustration, and feeling maxed out.

What do you sense when you look at this card?

....

....

....

Take a deep breath and sit back. Now tune into your inner experience. How are you feeling? Angry? Resentful? Like you are working too hard at something? Describe the situation.

....

....

....

....

....

What feelings do you need to express about this situation? Write it all out.

....

....

....

....

....

What constructive action steps can you take at this time? Make a list.

....

....

....

....

....

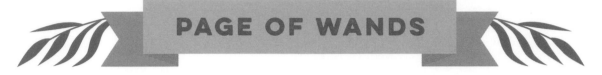

PAGE OF WANDS

The Page of Wands carries a bubbly, playful, expressive energy that is full of fun, creativity, and joy. It can represent a young person or a person with youthful qualities. It can also signify seeing these characteristics within yourself.

What do you sense when you look at this card?

....

....

....

In what areas of your life are you longing to lighten up and have more fun?

....

....

....

Write out three playful things you could do right now, even if it's just dancing in the living room.

....

....

....

....

....

Plan a fun outing, such as going to a concert or playing a sport, in detail, visualizing and describing all the best parts.

....

....

....

....

....

....

ASTROLOGICAL ASSOCIATIONS

The suit of Wands is associated with the fire signs: Aries, Leo, and Sagittarius. If one of its court cards indicates a person in your life, they likely are one of these signs or exhibit its characteristics.

KNIGHT OF WANDS

The Knight of Wands signifies powerful, dynamic forward motion. Nothing can stop you! It can represent a person with intense fire and focus. It can also signify seeing these characteristics within yourself.

What do you sense when you look at this card?

....

....

....

In what area(s) of your life do you need to move forward?

....

....

....

....

....

Are you feeling ready to go full speed ahead right now? If so, what are your plans? If not, how can you motivate yourself?

....

....

....

....

....

....

**Trust your energy at this time
and take some decisive action.**

QUEEN OF WANDS

The Queen of Wands is the feminine aspect of the fire element and signifies sharing and the spirit of generosity. It can represent a woman who is warm and expressive. It can also signify seeing these characteristics within yourself.

What do you sense when you look at this card?

....

....

....

Are you feeling full of energy and seeking a way to share it? In what ways could you do this now? Host a dinner party? Reach out to a friend? List them.

....

....

....

....

....

Think of a woman in your life with these qualities to whom you are drawn. What could you learn from her?

....

....

....

....

SHARE YOUR GIFTS

The Queen of Wands asks you to show up for others. When you share your talents and positivity, your energy grows.

KING OF WANDS

The King of Wands represents the mastery of fire—taking charge, exercising discipline in your actions, channeling creative energy in a constructive way. It can represent a man who has these qualities, or it can signify seeing these characteristics within yourself.

What do you sense when you look at this card?

....

....

....

Either stand up or sit with your back straight and your feet on the floor. Hold your hands in front of your chest, palms facing each other, 8 to 10 inches apart. Imagine a golden ball of light between your hands. This is your inner fire. Can you feel this energy? What does it feel like?

....

....

....

....

What does "taking charge" mean for you at this time?

....

....

....

....

What is it you want most right now? Write out a simple game plan, then commit to confidently putting it into action.

....

....

....

....

....

ACE OF CUPS

The Ace of Cups is the seed card of this suit. It represents a powerful inner sense of well-being and a clear, deep feeling of oneness, trusting both yourself and the Universe.

What do you sense when you look at this card?

....

....

....

Do you trust your connection with the Universe? Why or why not?

....

....

....

What do "inner faith" and "well-being" mean to you?

....

....

....

Repeat the mantra "All is well" to yourself—or write it down if that feels more powerful.

....

....

....

....

THE SUIT OF CUPS

The suit of Cups represents the water element. This suit of the heart deals with all aspects of feelings, emotions, and relationships.

TWO OF CUPS

The Two of Cups is about partnership—specifically, a deep loving relationship that is balanced and equitable.

What do you sense when you look at this card?

....

....

....

Are you seeking a loving relationship? Are you in one? Define the qualities of what a loving relationship means to you.

....

....

....

....

If married or in a committed partnership, what can you do to enhance or bring more love into the relationship?

....

....

....

....

....

When your faith in love is faltering, what can you do to restore or bolster it? (For example, you could look to a couple you admire or notice what is loving in yourself.)

....

....

....

....

....

THREE OF CUPS

The Three of Cups signifies a celebration of love, increased intimacy, and emotional connection with those around you.

What do you sense when you look at this card?

....

....

....

Think about a wedding or some other loving gathering coming up in your life. What are you looking forward to? Why?

....

....

....

....

....

How can you enjoy more connection with the people in your life to whom you feel drawn?

....

....

....

....

....

In what ways can you express more love in your daily life?

....

....

....

....

....

FOUR OF CUPS

The Four of Cups indicates the ability to seek out more equanimity through centering prayer, meditation, or any practice that drops you into your heart.

What do you sense when you look at this card?

....

....

....

Describe a practice that you are currently doing or that you'd like to try to help you feel calm and centered.

....

....

....

....

FINDING EQUIPOISE

The Four of Cups has an energy of detachment, but in a good way. You're finding balance and not tipping toward one specific feeling.

Think about a blessing in your life that you haven't recognized. Recognize it now. Write down what you appreciate about it.

....

....

....

....

List five things you are grateful for. Do you feel a shift in your energy?

....

....

....

....

....

....

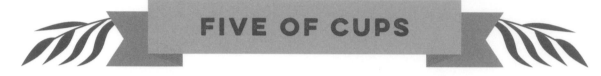

FIVE OF CUPS

The Five of Cups represents disappointments and feeling let down. It can also signify seeing what isn't working instead of seeing what is working.

What do you sense when you look at this card?

....

....

....

In what specific situation do you fear being disappointed? Why?

....

....

....

Try to identify areas where you might be seeing the glass as half empty instead of half full. How can you change your perspective?

....

....

....

What past disappointment do you still think or talk about? Write it down and then let it go to make space for a new experience.

....

....

....

"I believe in the magic of the cards to inspire us to let go of old ideas and restrictions."

—TONYA SHERIDAN

SIX OF CUPS

The Six of Cups carries the energy of nostalgia and looking at the past, either to childhood experiences or to an earlier relationship. You might be longing for an idealized version of love.

What do you sense when you look at this card?

....

....

....

How were your beliefs and feelings about love, family, or relationships forged by your past?

....

....

....

....

....

How can you update these beliefs and feelings? What would they look like?

....

....

....

....

....

How do you look to relationships—whether past, present, or what you hope for in the future—for fulfillment? How can you rely on yourself for more fulfillment now?

....

....

....

....

....

SEVEN OF CUPS

The Seven of Cups is associated with delusions or projecting emotions onto a situation or person. Look inward for clarity rather than outside of yourself.

What do you sense when you look at this card?

....

....

....

Take a deep breath. What areas of your life are lacking clarity right now? Put your hand on your heart and ask yourself, "How do I feel about this?" Write it out.

....

....

....

....

Are you trying to guess what someone in your life is feeling or how they perceive you? Do you feel like you might be projecting your own insecurities onto them? Why?

....

....

....

....

....

Identifying your own desires will bring clarity. Write out what you want to experience in a relationship. Then consider communicating this to your partner using "I feel" phrases and be willing to listen to how the other person feels.

....

....

....

....

EIGHT OF CUPS

The Eight of Cups is about letting go emotionally. It's time to move on from whatever feelings you have been holding on to and release the past.

What do you sense when you look at this card?

....

....

....

What situation in your life do you need to walk away from?

....

....

....

....

....

....

This card indicates a time of going forth into deeper emotional territory. Write about what that means for you in your present situation.

....

....

....

....

....

READY YOUR CUP

Letting go of what doesn't serve you doesn't leave your cup empty. Instead, it ensures positive things can keep flowing in.

The Nine of Cups is known as the "wish card." It tells you that you can trust in the manifestation of what your heart longs for.

What do you sense when you look at this card?

....

....

....

Write out a wish list. Don't think—just let your heart's desires pour onto the page.

....

....

....

....

....

....

....

If you suddenly found a magic lamp, and the genie popped out and said he would grant you one wish, which wish from your list would you choose?

....

....

....

Recall a time when you got something you wished for. Sit in that feeling and let it soften any doubts.

TEN OF CUPS

The Ten of Cups signifies emotional fulfillment. It indicates a time when love is overflowing from inside yourself to those around you.

What do you sense when you look at this card?

....

....

....

What does "emotional fulfillment" mean for you at this time?

....

....

....

....

....

Identify the relationships (with family, friends, or other loved ones) that feel really good right now. What about them is fulfilling?

....

....

....

....

....

Take a moment and place your hands on your heart. Breathe into this area. Now imagine this energy increasing and radiating out from you. How does that feel?

....

....

....

....

....

PAGE OF CUPS

The Page of Cups indicates playful emotional expression and allowing youthful, trusting energy to flow freely. It can represent a young person who is sweet and loving. It can also signify seeing these characteristics within yourself.

What do you sense when you look at this card?

....

....

....

How does it feel in your body when you allow yourself to trust?

....

....

....

Write about the areas in your life where it feels easier and more natural to follow your heart.

....

....

....

....

....

Repeat the mantra "It is safe to trust my heart" or write it down if that feels more powerful.

....

....

....

....

....

....

....

ASTROLOGICAL ASSOCIATIONS

The suit of Cups is associated with the water signs: Pisces, Cancer, and Scorpio. If one of its court cards indicates a person in your life, they likely are one of these signs or exhibit its characteristics.

KNIGHT OF CUPS

The Knight of Cups combines the action energy of a knight with emotions, signifying bravely following your desires and sending messages of love. It can represent a person with the qualities of intensity, deep feelings, and emotional expression, or it can represent seeing these characteristics within yourself.

What do you sense when you look at this card?

....

....

....

Has someone in your life recently expressed to you how they feel? How did it feel to receive that?

....

....

....

....

....

Have you ever experienced intense desire? How did it manifest?

....

....

....

....

....

What does it feel like to have your heart overtake your head?

....

....

....

....

....

The Queen of Cups signifies having a giving nature and being vulnerable, caring, and generous. It can represent a woman who has these sensitive and loving attributes as well as receptivity and openness. It can also signify seeing these characteristics within yourself.

What do you sense when you look at this card?

....

....

....

Think about a woman in your life to whom you are drawn who has these qualities. What could you learn from her?

....

....

....

....

....

What does it feel like when you are vulnerable and loving? Does it scare you? Can you see the strength in these qualities?

....

....

....

....

....

....

"As we journey inward, we reflect our light outward."

—BARON BAPTISTE

KING OF CUPS

The King of Cups heralds mastery of emotions and a healing, balanced, self-aware presence. It can represent a mature man who is in touch with his feelings and expresses them positively. It can also signify seeing these characteristics within yourself.

What do you sense when you look at this card?

....

....

....

How do you process your emotions? Easily? With difficulty? Why?

....

....

....

....

....

What current situation do you want to handle in a balanced, loving way? Write down some ways in which you think you can do that.

....

....

....

....

....

What does emotional maturity look like to you?

....

....

....

....

Creating Ritual and Intention

WHEN COMING TO THE TABLE TO WORK WITH TAROT and consciously activate your intuition, establishing a ritual is key. Doing this will signal to your mind that you are stepping out of your normal everyday consciousness and into a sacred space. The ritual itself will set you up for a productive and insightful reading. You will clear your reading space's energy, ground and protect yourself, open yourself to higher guidance, set your intention, and infuse the cards with this intention through shuffling. The following suggestions and exercises will help you create the ritual that is right for you, whether you are doing an intuitive reading for yourself or for others. But, don't worry, you can always change things up as both your practice and your intuition evolve.

> ## "The moment the senses start turning inward, we are tapping into the eternal source of energy."
>
> —GURUDEV SRI SRI RAVI SHANKAR

Setting Up Your Reading Space

Find a place in your home that you can set up as your reading space. This could be your dining room table, your desk, or any other space that you can convert into your reading zone as needed. It is best if you use the same place consistently. Some people even have a special tablecloth or scarf that they lay out before doing a reading.

Where will you create your reading space? How will you prepare it?

....

....

....

....

....

....

Clearing the Energy

You'll need to clear the energy in the room before a reading. You can do this using sage, palo santo, or incense. Simply light it and wave the smoke around the area you will work in. You can also light a candle before a reading to sanctify the space. (There is a reason most religions light candles or oil lamps in their sacred spaces.)

How will you clear your energetic space?

....

....

....

....

....

Connecting to Higher Guidance

Once your space is sanctified, you will want to open your energy field to receive guidance. For this, you can use a simple process called "connect, ground, protect." To do this, stand tall or sit in a chair with your spine straight and feet on the ground. Then visualize yourself immersed in a column of flowing white light as if you were standing in a waterfall. Connect to the light streaming from above you, bring it down all around you, and send it deep into the ground beneath you.

In only a few seconds, this exercise clears your energy field, connects you to the Universe—whatever that means for you personally—and grounds the energy while detaching and protecting you from outside influences. Try this now. Before you begin, take stock of how you feel and jot it down. Connected or disconnected? Focused or unfocused? Take three deep breaths and check in.

Write down how you feel now.

....

....

....

Once you've performed this exercise, take stock again. Do you feel different? Grounded? Connected? Open to receiving guidance? Write it down.

....

....

....

CONNECTING FOR OTHERS

You can also perform the "connect, ground, protect" process for another person. Simply imagine them in their own column of white light.

Dedicating Your Space

Dedicating your reading or any type of spiritual practice (e.g., yoga, meditation, or prayer) to another person, place in the world, or situation is not only altruistic, it will also strengthen the energy flowing through you. A catchall dedication that Buddhists use is to offer your practice to the upliftment of all beings from suffering.

How will you dedicate your readings?

....

....

....

....

Setting Your Intention

Setting an intention for your reading is very important. Having a specific question or area of your life that you wish to have guidance about helps avoid confusion and empathy overload. The clearer you are about what you are seeking guidance about, the clearer the guidance.

How will you ensure that your intention is clear and productive?

....

....

....

....

....

AN ALL-PURPOSE INTENTION

If you don't have a specific question, you can set an intention to be open to any messages that serve your highest good. You can also offer this intention when reading for others.

Shuffling

When reading for yourself, shuffle the cards, cut the deck into three piles with your left hand, and put them back into one pile in any order. If you're reading for someone else, and they are physically present, have them shuffle, cut, and stack the cards. If you are reading for someone remotely, follow the same steps as if reading for yourself, but with the intention that you are shuffling the deck to read for that person. The cards are now ready. Always take the top card and place it in order using the layout of your choice (see page 127 for more on layouts). Try this now and consider how your energy feels.

Do you feel a connection with the deck? Are you getting any impressions from it already? If so, what are they?

....

....

....

....

READING FOR OTHERS

Remember when you are reading for another person that the reading is providing information from their perspective, not your own. Stay as detached as possible. You are simply the messenger, accessing intuitive guidance and interpreting the cards for them.

Concluding the Ritual

After the reading, gather up the cards and shuffle the deck thoroughly. You may want to run the deck through the smoke of the sage or incense to cleanse the energy. Then clear your own energy field (especially important if reading for another person) by doing the "connect, ground, protect" process again. Blow out the candle and put your cards and accoutrements somewhere safe and private. Some people have a special cloth bag or lined box in which to keep their Tarot cards and other items for a reading. These are your sacred tools.

Where will you keep them? How will you keep them safe and protected?

....

....

....

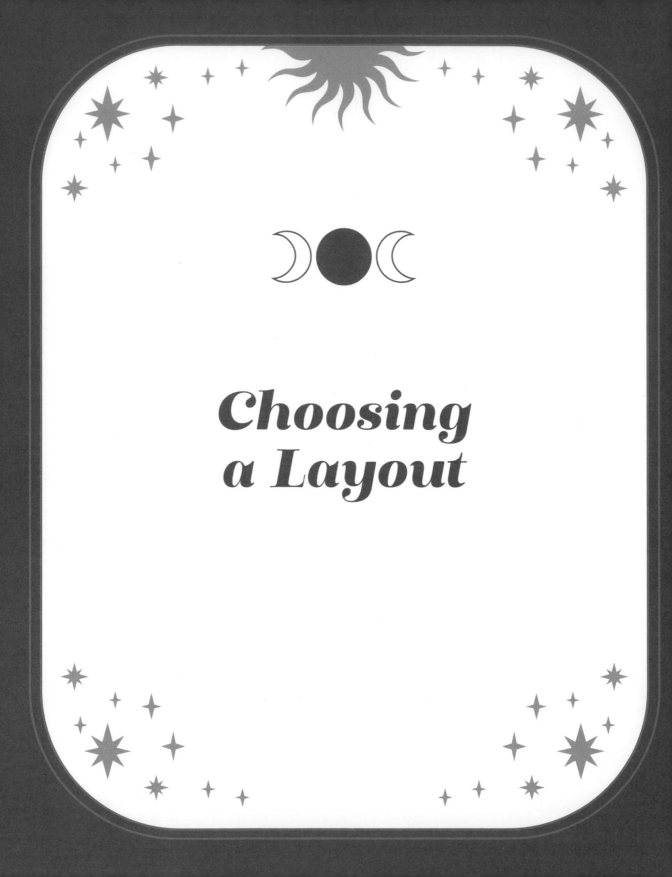

Choosing a Layout

UNDERSTANDING AND CHOOSING A LAYOUT

(aka spread) is a very important component of reading Tarot. The layouts are the templates we use to understand the context of the cards.

The following descriptions and exercises will give you some basic layouts to work with. You'll start with the simplest, the one-card reading, and work up to the most complex, the Celtic Cross spread.

Each layout has its own strengths. More complex does not mean better, just more detailed. Sometimes less is more. The most important thing is to choose the layout that will be the most helpful for you, and that means understanding them intuitively. It doesn't matter whether you approach the following exercises in order or choose to repeat one over and over until you feel proficient. The most essential aspect of learning how to understand layouts is also the most enjoyable: practice, practice, practice!

In this section, you'll practice tapping into your intuition in relation to the cards and their placements. This lays the foundation for what comes next: interpreting the cards. For now, just focus on deepening your energetic connection with the cards in layout form.

BEFORE YOU BEGIN

Before a reading, simply shuffle the deck—always face down—
and pull the cards one at a time from the top of the deck, placing
them face up in the positions indicated by the layout.

The One-Card Reading

You can use the one-card reading either to answer a very specific question that you have on a single topic or to simply receive guidance for the day.

Set your intention. Shuffle the deck, take the top card, turn it over, and observe.

1

CORE
MESSAGE

YOUR CARD

....

What is your first reaction to this card?

....

....

....

....

Stay out of your head. Write down what you see, hear, and feel.

....

....

....

....

What colors, symbols, and visual narratives come to you?

....

....

....

....

Do you hear any guidance? If so, what?

....

....

....

....

What sounds, songs, or words come to you as you study this card?

....

....

....

....

Take a deep breath and tune into your feeling sense. What emotions does this card evoke? Do you notice any sensations in your body?

....

....

....

....

....

The Three-Card Spread

This layout is building on the one-card reading. It gives you a larger context and more information that can illuminate the message of the central card. The first card you pull is the central theme. The second card (placed to the left) indicates the influence of the recent past. The third card (placed to the right) is the future trajectory.

Set your intention. After shuffling the deck and placing the three cards, sit back and just observe them together.

2	1	3
PAST	CORE MESSAGE	FUTURE

YOUR CARDS

1: ....

2: ....

3: ....

What comes to you about this combination of cards? Just write any thoughts that come to mind, staying in the stream of consciousness.

CARD #1: THE CORE MESSAGE

Now focus on the middle card, which gives you the central theme of the reading. What do you see, hear, and feel? Write about whatever comes to you.

Visual Impressions

....

....

....

....

....

Audio Impressions

....

....

....

....

....

Physical Sensations

....

....

....

....

....

Feelings or Emotions

....

....

....

....

....

CARD #2: THE PAST

Next, focus on the card to the left, which represents the past influences related to the central theme. What do you see, hear, and feel? Write about whatever comes to you.

Visual Impressions

....

....

....

....

....

Audio Impressions

....

....

....

....

....

Physical Sensations

....

....

....

....

....

Feelings or Emotions

....

....

....

....

....

CARD #3: THE FUTURE

Finally, look at the card to the right, which signifies the future trajectory related to the past influences and central theme. What do you see, hear, and feel? Write about whatever comes to you.

Visual Impressions

....

....

....

....

....

Audio Impressions

....

....

....

....

....

Physical Sensations

....

....

....

....

....

Feelings or Emotions

....

....

....

....

....

The V Spread

The V Spread is very good to use when you have a specific question and are looking for as much information as possible about that topic. The way to do that is to always come back to the core message, which is illustrated by the very shape of the V Spread.

To create this spread, set your intention, shuffle the deck, and lay out the cards as shown: Place the first card at the top left of the V. The next card goes below it on a diagonal line. The third card is placed below that. The fourth card is the bottom point of the V. The fifth card goes up the diagonal line to the right. The sixth goes above that. And the seventh card sits at the top of the line on the right. This creates a V shape with the central message as the point.

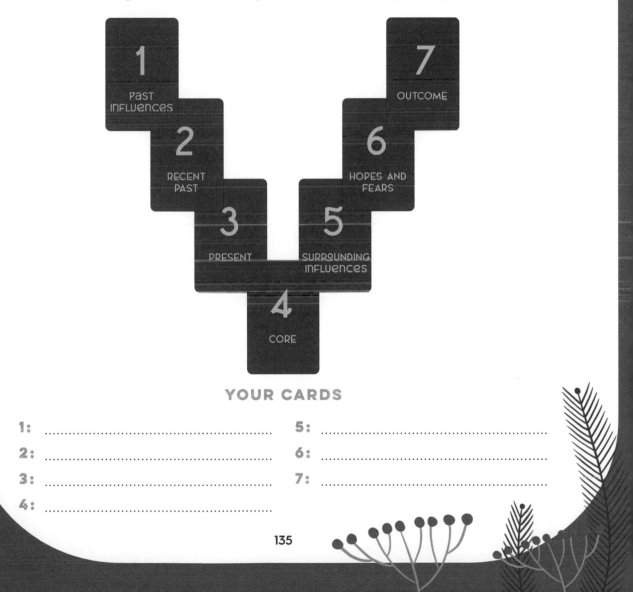

YOUR CARDS

1: ....

2: ....

3: ....

4: ....

5: ....

6: ....

7: ....

Before you go into reading each placement, sit back and just take in the layout. Write out any impressions that come to you.

....

....

....

....

....

....

....

....

....

....

....

....

....

....

....

....

....

....

....

INFORMATION OVERLOAD

It is important to note that seeking more information can be confusing. There is a tendency to overthink it all. If you feel this is happening, sit back, take a breath, and just use the simplest meaning of the card in its placement.

CARD #1: PAST INFLUENCES

This is the past as pertains to the central theme. What do you see, hear, feel when you look at this card? Write about your impressions.

Visual Impressions

....

....

....

....

....

Audio Impressions

....

....

....

....

....

Physical Sensations

....

....

....

....

....

Feelings or Emotions

....

....

....

....

....

CARD #2: THE RECENT PAST

This placement shows what you've just been experiencing. What do you see, hear, and feel? Write about your impressions.

Visual Impressions

....

....

....

....

....

Audio Impressions

....

....

....

....

....

Physical Sensations

....

....

....

....

....

Feelings or Emotions

....

....

....

....

....

CARD #3: THE PRESENT

This card represents the present as it pertains to the central theme. What do you see, hear, and feel? Write about your impressions.

Visual Impressions

....

....

....

....

....

Audio Impressions

....

....

....

....

....

Physical Sensations

....

....

....

....

....

Feelings or Emotions

....

....

....

....

....

CARD #4: THE CORE MESSAGE

This card offers guidance about the central theme regarding your specific question. Take a moment and really sit with this one. What do you see, hear, and feel? Write about your impressions.

Visual Impressions

....
....
....
....
....

Audio Impressions

....
....
....
....
....

Physical Sensations

....
....
....
....
....

Feelings or Emotions

....
....
....
....
....

CARD #5: SURROUNDING INFLUENCES

This placement reflects your environment at this time and the influences that surround you regarding your question. What do you see, hear, and feel? Write about your impressions.

Visual Impressions

....
....
....
....
....

Audio Impressions

....
....
....
....
....

Physical Sensations

....
....
....
....
....

Feelings or Emotions

....
....
....
....
....

CARD #6: HOPES AND FEARS

This card represents your hopes and/or fears regarding your question. What does this card say to you? What do you see, hear, and feel? Write about your impressions.

Visual Impressions

....

....

....

....

....

Audio Impressions

....

....

....

....

....

Physical Sensations

....

....

....

....

....

Feelings or Emotions

....

....

....

....

....

This card shows the future trajectory based on all the other cards. Focus on this card, then write out your impressions. Again, what do you see, hear, and feel?

Visual Impressions

....

....

....

Audio Impressions

....

....

....

Physical Sensations

....

....

....

Feelings or Emotions

....

....

....

REPETITION BOOSTS INTUITION

Although the exercises for each card may seem redundant, they are essential. If you keep bringing your attention to what you see, hear, and feel, you will soon find your senses heightened. This develops your extrasensory perception, which allows your intuition to come through.

The Relationship Spread

The Relationship Spread is ideal for understanding the dynamic between you and another person. It shines light on the energy around you and the other person, as well as the energy between you, and offers guidance for the situation.

To create this spread, set your intention, shuffle the deck, and lay out the cards as illustrated: Place the first card to the left and the second card next to it on the right. The third card goes beneath the first card, and the last card goes next to it at the bottom right.

1	2
YOU	THEM

3	4
YOUR RELATIONSHIP	THE GUIDANCE (CORE MESSAGE)

YOUR CARDS

1: ....

2: ....

3: ....

4: ....

Before you go into reading each placement, sit back and just take in the layout. Write out any impressions that come to you.

CARD #1: YOU

This card represents the energy you are bringing to the relationship. What do you see, hear, and feel when you look at this card? Write about your impressions.

Visual Impressions

....
....
....
....
....

Audio Impressions

....
....
....
....
....

Physical Sensations

....
....
....
....
....

Feelings or Emotions

....
....
....
....
....

CARD #2: THEM

This card shows you what is going on with the other person. Detach as much as possible, then write about your impressions. What do you see, hear, and feel?

Visual Impressions

....

....

....

....

....

Audio Impressions

....

....

....

....

....

Physical Sensations

....

....

....

....

....

Feelings or Emotions

....

....

....

....

....

CARD #3: YOUR RELATIONSHIP

This card represents the dynamic between the two of you and can be very revealing, so take the time to feel into it. What do you see, hear, and feel? Write about your impressions.

Visual Impressions

....

....

....

....

....

Audio Impressions

....

....

....

....

....

Physical Sensations

....

....

....

....

....

Feelings or Emotions

....

....

....

....

....

CARD #4: THE CORE MESSAGE

This card offers you the guidance you're seeking. What are your impressions? Again, write about what you see, hear, and feel.

Visual Impressions

....

....

....

Audio Impressions

....

....

....

Physical Sensations

....

....

....

Feelings or Emotions

....

....

....

"If you knew your potential to feel good, you would ask no one to be different so that you can feel good."

—ESTHER HICKS

The Celtic Cross Spread

The Celtic Cross is the layout that most professional Tarot readers use. It is a comprehensive template that really gives you the lay of the land. This spread has ten placements, and it is important to learn each placement to avoid confusion. Just take it one step at a time and allow the cards to speak to you. After creating the layout and noting your intuitive impressions about each card, sit back and take a wide-angle view of the reading. This will help you perceive the overall feeling of the spread.

Set your intention, shuffle the deck, and lay out the cards as illustrated: Place the first card in the center and the second card horizontally across the first card, forming a plus sign. The third card goes above the plus sign and the fourth card goes underneath it. Place the fifth card to the left of the plus sign and the sixth card to the right of it. That forms the basic cross. The last four cards go in a column to the right of the cross, starting with the seventh at the bottom and then placing the eighth, ninth, and tenth cards in a line going up.

TAKE YOUR TIME

This is a large layout, so make sure you leave enough room to spread the cards out and take everything in. Working one section at a time can help you avoid overwhelm. Start by understanding the cross section, then work through the column before zooming out to see how they work together.

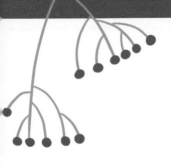

3

CONSCIOUS
THOUGHTS

10

OUTCOME
(CORE
MESSAGE)

5

RECENT
PAST

2

OBSTACLE OR
OPPORTUNITY

1: THE SITUATION

6

NEAR
FUTURE

9

HOPES AND
FEARS

8

OUTER
INFLUENCES

4

UNCONSCIOUS
THOUGHTS

7

FUTURE

YOUR CARDS

1: ....   6: ....

2: ....   7: ....

3: ....   8: ....

4: ....   9: ....

5: ....   10: ....

CARD 1: THE SITUATION

This card's placement indicates where you are now. What do you see, hear, and feel when you look at this card? Write about your impressions.

Visual Impressions

....

....

....

....

....

Audio Impressions

....

....

....

....

....

Physical Sensations

....

....

....

....

....

Feelings or Emotions

....

....

....

....

CARD 2: OBSTACLE OR OPPORTUNITY

This card represents what is "crossing" you. It is either an obstacle or an opportunity, depending on the card. Turn this card from horizontal to vertical and look at it. What is it trying to tell you? What do you see, hear, and feel? Write about your impressions.

Visual Impressions

....

....

....

....

....

Audio Impressions

....

....

....

....

....

Physical Sensations

....

....

....

....

....

Feelings or Emotions

....

....

....

....

CARD 3: CONSCIOUS THOUGHTS

This card shows you what is going on in your conscious, analytical mind. What do you see, hear, and feel? Write about your impressions.

Visual Impressions

....
....
....
....

Audio Impressions

....
....
....
....

Physical Sensations

....
....
....
....

Feelings or Emotions

....
....
....

Do these impressions make sense to you?

....
....
....
....

CARD 4: SUBCONSCIOUS THOUGHTS

This position represents your subconscious influences. It is important because it gives you insight into things you are normally unaware of but are influencing your perspective. Again, write about your impressions. What do you see, hear, and feel?

Visual Impressions

....

....

....

....

....

Audio Impressions

....

....

....

....

....

Physical Sensations

....

....

....

....

....

Feelings or Emotions

....

....

....

....

CARD 5: RECENT PAST

This placement represents the recent past. It gives you insight into how your past is influencing your present. What do you see, hear, and feel? Write about your impressions.

Visual Impressions

....

....

....

....

....

Audio Impressions

....

....

....

....

....

Physical Sensations

....

....

....

....

....

Feelings or Emotions

....

....

....

....

....

CARD 6: NEAR FUTURE

This card represents the near future and how you can move forward. What do you see, hear, and feel? Write about your impressions.

Visual Impressions

....
....
....
....
....

Audio Impressions

....
....
....
....
....

Physical Sensations

....
....
....
....
....

Feelings or Emotions

....
....
....
....
....

CARD 7: FUTURE

This position is interesting because it indicates the stance you'll take in the future based on where you are now. What do you see, hear, and feel when you look at this card? Write about your impressions.

Visual Impressions

....

....

....

....

....

Audio Impressions

....

....

....

....

....

Physical Sensations

....

....

....

....

....

Feelings or Emotions

....

....

....

....

....

CARD 8: OUTER INFLUENCES

This indicates the environment surrounding you in the near future and how it impacts you. What do you see, hear, and feel? Write about your impressions.

Visual Impressions

....
....
....
....
....

Audio Impressions

....
....
....
....
....

Physical Sensations

....
....
....
....
....

Feelings or Emotions

....
....
....
....
....

CARD 9: HOPES AND FEARS

This placement represents your future hopes and fears. It gives you insight into what you'll be thinking. What is this card saying to you? What do you see, hear, and feel? Write about your impressions.

Visual Impressions

....
....
....
....
....

Audio Impressions

....
....
....
....
....

Physical Sensations

....
....
....
....
....

Feelings or Emotions

....
....
....
....
....

CARD 10: CORE MESSAGE

This final card is traditionally called the "outcome card." It represents what you can expect based on your current trajectory and can give you key guidance about your question. Again, write down your impressions. What do you see, hear, and feel?

Visual Impressions

....
....
....
....
....

Audio Impressions

....
....
....
....
....

Physical Sensations

....
....
....
....
....

Feelings or Emotions

....
....
....
....

Clarifying Cards

If you find the outcome card disturbing, don't stop there. Pull one or two more cards for guidance on how you can work constructively with the energy of the outcome card. Write out the impressions that come to you until you feel a sense of completeness.

....
....
....
....
....
....
....
....
....
....
....
....
....
....
....
....
....
....
....
....
....
....

Final Impressions

Now sit back, take a deep breath, and take in the whole spread. This layout is telling you a story. It has a beginning, a middle, and an end. It is giving you guidance and activating your intuition so you have information that can help you. As you look at its narrative, can you sense this? Write out any thoughts and feelings that the overall layout evokes in you.

....

....

....

....

....

....

....

....

....

....

....

....

....

....

"Don't try to comprehend with your mind. Your minds are very limited. Use your intuition."

—MADELEINE L'ENGLE

Interpreting the Cards

NOW THAT YOU'VE EXERCISED YOUR INTUITION muscles, we're going to incorporate what you've learned about the arcanas, suits, and court cards. You always want to start with your intuition—letting the imagery of the cards provoke your inner awareness is key. However, Tarot also has a clear structure. The twenty-two themes of the major arcana are organized to follow the Fool's journey from start to finish, each step building on the last. The minor arcana is divided into four distinct elements that make up our life experiences. The court cards represent people of different temperaments and ages. So bringing this knowledge to the reading is going to support what your intuition is telling you.

The definitions of the cards provide the framework, giving structure to the sometimes amorphous feelings of intuition while stabilizing what you see, hear, or feel about each card. This will aid you in getting more specific guidance. But because most people are so used to their logical, analytical minds running the show, it is important to keep this in check. Don't get lost in your head! Stay with your inner senses as you check in with the cards' meanings. You'll find that these aspects harmonize and bring you really helpful guidance.

This chapter will help you trust your interpretations of the individual cards, build your repertoire, and synthesize layouts. You will use the three-card spread for these exercises, but you can expound on this process for more complex layouts using the pages at the back of the book. For the purpose of going deeper into interpreting the cards, you may want to go back and review your previous impressions of them. Learning and intuiting seventy-eight cards is a big job, so use what you have already gleaned to support this process.

EXTRA CREDIT

If you're struggling to remember your intuitive associations, you can always make flash cards. On each card, write the name of the Tarot card and then the core feelings and impressions that stand out to you about that card. This is not necessary or for everyone, but it can be a very helpful learning tool.

Synthesis

Set your intention, shuffle the deck, and lay out the cards as you did on page 130: place the first card in the center, the second card to the left, and the third card to the right. The first card represents the central theme, the second card signifies the past influences coming to bear on that theme, and the third card indicates the future trajectory.

FIRST IMPRESSIONS

The first thing to do is sit back and take a wide-angle view of the whole layout. What are your immediate impressions? Write them down.

....

....

....

Now take note of any major arcana cards. How many are there? In what positions? Remember, the major arcana cards represent overarching themes and longer time spans, so they should always stand out in a reading. If there are a lot of majors in a spread, then you know you are in a time of great growth and awareness that will have a lasting effect.

....

....

....

If the cards are from the minor arcana, you know the guidance is situational and specific. But the next step is to notice if there is a preponderance of one suit. If so, which suit is it? This is important—it will tell you the nature of the guidance. Cups signify feelings, pentacles indicate material reality, swords represent thoughts and beliefs, and wands are about action. What do your cards indicate?

....

....

....

....

CARD #1: THE CORE MESSAGE

Once you're finished with your initial impressions, focus on the center card (representing the main theme of the reading). Start by writing down your initial impressions of this card.

....

....

....

....

Is this card from the major arcana? The minor arcana? Is it a court card? Which suit is it? What does this say about the card?

....

....

....

....

....

Considering your impressions, the card's meaning, and its placement, what guidance do you get from this card?

....

....

....

....

....

YOUR ENERGY

If there is a court card in the #1 position,
and you are reading for yourself, this card
describes your energy at this time.

CARD #2: THE PAST

Now look at the card to the left. This placement represents the recent past. Start by writing down your initial impressions of this card.

....

....

....

Is this card from the major arcana? The minor arcana? Is it a court card? Which suit is it? What does this say about the card? (For example, a major arcana card indicates a longer time frame and a larger theme.)

....

....

....

....

....

If this is a court card, feel into this card. Does it represent a person in your life with these characteristics or an aspect of yourself?

....

....

....

....

....

Considering your impressions, the card's meaning, and its placement, what guidance do you get from this card?

....

....

....

....

CARD #3: THE FUTURE

Take a look at the card to the right. This card indicates the future. Start by writing down your initial impressions of this card.

....

....

....

Is this card from the major arcana? The minor arcana? Is it a court card? Which suit is it? What does this say about the card? A major arcana card in the future position, for example, means that either its overarching theme will be present in your life for a while or it offers a powerful message about what you are coming into.

....

....

....

....

....

If this is a court card, feel into this card. Does it represent a person in your life with these characteristics, or an aspect of yourself?

....

....

....

....

Considering your impressions, the card's meaning, and its placement, what guidance do you get from this card?

....

....

....

....

....

The Big Picture

There is an art to bringing all the cards in a reading together. You need a delicate balance, taking into account the individual cards but also allowing the narrative of the combination of cards to shine through. (The more comfortable you become with the individual cards, the easier this gets.) So, after answering all of the questions for each card, sit back and look at the layout.

Do certain colors, symbols, or characters stand out? Be open to your intuition and write what you see, hear, and feel.

As you look at the cards in the context of the overall timeline—from past to present to future—
what messages come to you?

....

....

....

....

....

....

....

....

....

....

....

....

....

....

....

....

....

....

....

....

"Tarot's purpose is to help you probe your own subconscious and to find answers within yourself."

—SKYE ALEXANDER

Keep Practicing

Take this process into any layout you choose to work with. Obviously, the bigger layouts will entail more synthesis as you combine all the cards' meanings with their placements, but the process is the same. Soon you will find it comes naturally. It's like learning how to drive: At first, maneuvering the car and abiding by the rules of the road take effort. But, after some practice, you will do it without thinking because you've internalized the process.

DATE: ....

INTENTION:

....

....

....

....

....

....

....

....

TYPE OF SPREAD: ....

CARDS PULLED

1: ....
2: ....
3: ....
4: ....
5: ....

6: ....
7: ....
8: ....
9: ....
10: ....

IMPRESSIONS

....
....
....
....
....
....
....
....
....
....

INTERPRETATION

....
....
....
....
....
....
....
....
....
....
....

DATE: ....

INTENTION:

....

....

....

....

....

....

....

....

....

....

....

....

....

....

....

....

TYPE OF SPREAD: ....

CARDS PULLED

1: .... 6: ....

2: .... 7: ....

3: .... 8: ....

4: .... 9: ....

5: .... 10: ....

IMPRESSIONS

....
....
....
....
....
....
....
....
....
....

INTERPRETATION

....
....
....
....
....
....
....
....
....
....

Congratulations!

This has been a big journey, but you have made it to the end. Time to pat yourself on the back! Give yourself some respect for delving into your own thoughts, feelings, and sensory perceptions. Many people won't even go there—*there* being inside themselves. Opening up to the shadows and the light of your consciousness takes a brave soul. But what other journey is more important? The more we understand ourselves, the more we can truly understand others. When we bring detachment and non-judgment to our own inner processes, we can then provide a safe space for others, in readings and in life.

Tuning into how you are feeling and what you are seeing and hearing builds self-awareness. This is the gateway to intuition. Using the rich iconography of Tarot is a wonderful tool to activate the wealth of inner guidance that is already inside you. And the more you practice, the clearer the guidance becomes, the easier it is to access it, and the more you'll trust it. May the merit of this process bring you into greater alignment with your spirit, bringing you happiness and fulfillment. And may that benefit you and all beings!

"The universe is full of magical things, patiently waiting for our wits to grow sharper."

—EDEN PHILLPOTTS